CW00341459

THE
LITTLE HONEY
BOOK

Mavis Budd

PIATKUS

Other titles in the series

The Little Green Avocado Book
The Little Garlic Book
The Little Pepper Book
The Little Apple Book
The Little Strawberry Book
The Little Lemon Book
The Little Bean Book
The Little Nut Book
The Little Mushroom Book
The Little Mustard Book
The Little Rice Book

©1984 Judy Piatkus (Publishers) Limited
First published in 1984 by Judy Piatkus
(Publishers) Limited of London

British Library Cataloguing in Publication Data
Budd, Mavis
The little honey book.
1. Honey
I. Title
641.3'8   SF539
ISBN 0-86188-459-0

Drawings by Linda Broad
Designed by Ken Leeder
Cover photograph by John Lee

Typeset by Gilbert Composing Services
Printed and bound by
The Pitman Press · Bath

CONTENTS

How doth the little busy bee
Improve each shining hour,
And gather honey all the day
From every opening flower.

How skilfully she builds her cell!
How neat she spreads the wax;
And labours hard to store it well
With the sweet food she makes.

Isaac Watts (1674–1748)

WHAT IS HONEY?

Honey is a sweet, viscous liquid created by honey bees from the nectar of flowering plants and trees.

It is the food provided by the bees for their own consumption and to feed their young. The honey not eaten in the hive during the season is stored away in cells in the combs for later use and as food for the winter when no nectar is available. The honey taken from the hive by bee-keepers is the excess which is not required by the bees.

Honey is a pure, natural food, delicious to eat and extremely nutritious, a beautifier and a healer and completely free of bacteria. It should be included in everyone's diet.

One pound of honey generates about 1,400 calories after being eaten and converted into energy and carbon dioxide.

Chemists have succeeded in discovering the exact composition but no one has been able to re-create honey chemically, and it is doubtful that anyone ever will. The creation of honey belongs exclusively to the bee.

An average sample of honey contains:

Moisture	17.0%
Levulose (d-fructose)	39.0%
Dextrose (d-glucose)	34.0%
Sucrose	1.0%
Dextrin	0.5%
Proteins	2.0%
Wax	1.0%
Plant acids	0.5%
Mineral salts	1.0%
Gums, resins, pollen grains, etc	4.0%

Among the vitamins in honey are: Thiamin (B1), Riboflavin (B2), B6, H, K, C and Niacin. The amounts, however, are likely to be small and not of great nutritional value.

The most important sugars in honey are: glucose, fructose and sucrose.

Glucose is the simplest of sugars and is found in fruit and the juices of plants. It helps to restore energy by providing the oxygen that is replaced by lactic acid when fatigue sets in.

Fructose, also called Levulose, is used by nature for building tissue.

Sucrose is a combination of glucose and fructose.

Dextrin, also found in honey, is a valuable constituent as it goes straight into the bloodstream and does not need to be digested.

The mineral salts include: potassium, calcium, iron chloride, magnesium, silicon, sodium, silica, manganese, sulphur, copper and phosphorous.

Filtered or over-refined honey may look attractive but it lacks many of the most valuable constituents, including the pollen grains which contain most of the vitamins and the mysterious properties which are reputed to prolong life.

HONEYDEW

Honeydew, a sweet, sticky substance, is created by aphids which suck the juices of trees, especially the sycamore, oak or plum, and excrete a sugary liquid which is a modified form of the tree's sap. Honeydew honey is produced chiefly in Eastern European countries, such as Bulgaria and Greece, where the climate is hot and dry, and the aphids living on the pines create a great deal of honeydew. The bees collect this almost exclusively, and the honey they create from it has a very good flavour.

There is very little honeydew honey produced in Britain. If there is insufficient nectar in the flowers of certain plants or trees, then the bees will work the aphids. The presence of honeydew in a comb will make the honey cloudy, thus spoiling it for showing, but not for eating.

THE HONEY BEE

Honey is made by the honey bee, *Apis mellifera*, and stored in six-sided cells in wax combs which are also made by the bee, the wax being produced from glands on the underside of its body, chewed until soft, then placed in position on the comb.

The honey is made from nectar, a sweet liquid consisting of sugars dissolved in water, which is produced by flowering plants to attract insects so that pollination can occur. Having sucked up the nectar, the worker bee carries it in her stomach back to the hive, where a house bee processes it by reducing the water content and adding enzymes before storing it in the wax cells to ripen.

Pollen adheres to the bee's body as she forages in the flowers and after being cleaned off, is stored in special pollen 'baskets' on her hind legs, carried back with the nectar and also passed to the waiting house bee, who packs it into storage cells, ready to feed to the young bees and to provide them with the protein which is essential to their health.

THE QUEEN BEE

Life in the hive is a well-organised, close-knit little society presided over by the queen who does nothing but lay eggs. A queen in the course of her life can produce well over a million eggs. She lays one in each cell of the comb and after three days the tiny larvae hatch. For three days they are fed on the white milky substance known as 'Royal Jelly', which is produced in the head glands of the house bee, then for the next two days on pollen and nectar. On the eighth day the cell in which the larva rests is capped with wax and it changes to a pupa. After twenty-one days it chews through the cap and emerges as an adult bee. The larva of a worker bee can be changed into a queen if it is fed on Royal Jelly for the duration of its five-day larval life instead of for only three days.

When a week-old queen emerges from her cell, she flies out of the hive to join the drones, or males, which circle it. Mating takes place and the queen settles back in the hive to spend the rest of her life producing eggs.

DRONES

Drones are the male bees. They have no facilities for carrying honey to the hive and are fed by the worker bees. The number of drones is restricted by the worker bees, who kill them when the flow of honey diminishes at the end of the season.

THE WORKER BEE

A worker bee spends the first three days of her life cleaning cells ready for the queen's eggs and feeding on honey and pollen stored in the comb. From the fourth to the ninth day, she takes care of the larvae, producing the Royal Jelly from her head glands, and also making 'bee bread', which is a mixture of honey and pollen, to feed to the older larvae.

At the end of this phase, the wax glands on her abdomen become active and for the next ten to sixteen days she builds combs and cells. From the seventeenth to the nineteenth day, she takes in the nectar and pollen loads from the foragers and processes them ready to store in the cells.

On day twenty she commences work as a guard bee, protecting the hive from intruders.

On day twenty-one till the end of her life, she goes out to forage for nectar and pollen and will probably die after only a few weeks in the open, though bees reared in the autumn who do not have to work so hard can live for as many as six or seven months.

SWARMING

Swarming is the only natural method of perpetuating the bee species and is a natural instinct in all bees. It is a form of colonising and can be to some extent prevented by providing more space for the bees to store nectar and by wet weather conditions.

A swarm is between 5 and 6 lbs in weight and contains approximately 20,000 bees.

TYPES OF HONEY

Honey is not a uniform product and therefore its nutritional value will vary from one honey to another, depending on the season, weather conditions, the plants from which the nectar has been collected, the soil in which the plants grew and, of course, the health of the bees and the care they received from the apiarist. Thus, the honey produced in one year will not be the same as honey produced in another, even if it has been made from the nectar of the same species of plant.

The colour of honey varies from water-white through amber, to dark brown. Some can be almost black. The darker the honey is, the more minerals and plant acids it will contain. Light coloured honey has a delicate flavour; darker ones are stronger.

As different plants and flowers yield different nectars, the honey from each one will have its own individual texture, aroma and flavour.

Because there are so few areas where a single plant species is growing, most of the honey produced in Britain is blended from the nectars of different plants. This gives it a special and subtle quality which cannot be achieved simply by mixing several types together.

An exception to these bee-blended honeys is:

HEATHER (LING) HONEY: there are large areas, such as Dartmoor, where the bees are able to work in heather alone and the honey produced has a unique distinctive flavour and quality. It is dark in colour with a strong flavour. Its texture is thick and jelly-like. It will liquefy when stirred but quickly return to its thick consistency when left to stand. The air bubbles, which form during the process of extracting the honey from the comb, are trapped by the dense consistency and give it a characteristic appearance.

The bell heather yields a different honey, which is rather reddish in colour and not gelatinous, though the flavour and aroma are good.

Among other honeys produced from a single plant in Britain are clover, lime, sainfoin, charlock, and sycamore, though in each one there is bound to be mingled some honey from other plants. Thus if a pot of honey is labelled 'Clover', 'Lime', and so on, this means that it has been produced mainly from these plants but will also include a little from others.

CLOVER is one of the favourite British honeys. It is light in colour with a delicate flavour and aroma. It sets with a smooth, fine grain.

LIME honey is slightly greenish, less dense than clover, and with a faint peppermint flavour.

SAINFOIN is a bright, sparkling, deep yellow honey.

CHARLOCK honey is light with a strong, rather pungent, flavour which mellows with time and granulates rapidly.

SYCAMORE honey has a greenish tinge. It granulates slowly and produces a coarse grain. This honey is not at its best when fresh.

ROSE BAY WILLOW HERB, sometimes called 'fire weed', is another honey-producing plant prevalent in some parts of the country, providing a good flow of late honey which is water-white and very sweet. Having no distinctive flavour, it is useful for blending with stronger honeys.

Among other wild plants in Britain which produce honey in quantity are the hawthorn, blackberry, dandelion and raspberry.

FLOWERS SPECIALLY FAVOURED BY THE BEES

Among the important honey plants which grow in Britain month by month are the following:

January: None

February–March: Celandine, coltsfoot, crocus, violet, snowdrop

April: Plum, cherry and pear blossom

May: Dandelion, hawthorn, apple blossom, forget-me-not, sycamore, gorse, wallflowers

June: Raspberry, sainfoin, clover, beans, vetches

July: White clover, blackberry, limes, willow herb, hogweed, lavender

July–August: Willow herb, bell heather, lime, red clover, Himalayan balsam

August–September: Ling heather, mustard, Himalayan balsam, thistles, meadow sweet

September–October: Ling heather, mustard, Michaelmas daisies, thistles, white charlock

November–December: None

In honey-producing countries where there are extensive areas of single-type plants and trees, the honey is more uniform.

* In Australia there are gum trees, box and iron-barks; the clover, lucerne and Salvation Jane.

* In the United States there are the citrus trees of California and Florida.

* New Zealand has its flowering trees, berry fruits, Kiwi fruits and other fruit blossoms.

* In Russia there are vast crops of buckwheat.

* In South-East Europe the acacias produce a special brand of honey.

* All round the Mediterranean there are the mountain flowers, the wild lavender, rosemary, herbs and the olive trees.

THE TASTE OF HONEY

All honey is sweet but due to the different sugars in nectar some will taste sweeter than others. The sugar content in nectar varies from between 3% to over 80% though most contain about 40% or perhaps a little less.

Among the plants that produce very sweet honey are the acacias of South-East Europe. The nectar of acacia contains about 60% sugar.

Other plants which provide sweet honey are sainfoin, thistle and Himalayan balsam which spread through Europe and Britain during the 1960s, establishing itself as a wild plant of river banks and damp places, and became a great favourite of the bees.

The substances—sometimes in minute amounts—which contribute to the individual flavours of different honeys include the sugars, amino acids, proline, tannins, glucosides and alkaloidal compounds.

The taste of honey is closely linked to the aroma and this again varies from one honey to another. An expert honey-taster can usually detect the single plant source by its scent. Among honeys with

definite aromas are rosemary honey from the
Mediterranean countries, thyme honey from
Greece, orange blossom honey from Spain and
heather honey from Britain and Europe.

Both flavour and aroma are at their best when the
honey is first taken from the hive.

GETTING HONEY
OUT OF THE
COMB

In primitive times the honeycomb was simply
broken apart so that the honey could run out into
a container, after which it was strained through a
cloth into storage containers. The remaining
fragments of wax and other bits left in the cloth were
used to make honey drinks such as mead.

The extraction of honey today is a highly
developed operation. Equipment is sophisticated
and efficient and the honey is carefully graded and
packaged. After the wax cappings on the comb have
been removed with a specially designed revolving

blade, the combs are placed in a rapidly revolving basket from which the honey is thrown clear by centrifugal force. It is then strained and left to stand while the air bubbles rise. Surface bubbles are skimmed off and the honey is stored ready for bottling. The empty combs are returned to the bee hives where the bees set about cleaning them and repairing any damaged cells ready to be refilled.

A backyard bee-keeper with a few hives uses a similar method to extract his honey but on a much smaller scale. He removes the wax cappings with a uncapping knife, then places the comb in a mesh basket in a honey-extractor. This is a tall cylinder with a handle which turns the basket so that the honey is thrown out by centrifugal force and drips down the sides of the cylinder. The honey is then run into a honey tank where it passes through a filter before being run off by a little tap into jars or containers.

The standard colours and descriptions of honey vary from country to country, but in Britain the colours of honey for sale are Select Light Colour; Select Medium Colour; Select Dark Colour. These are determined by standard colour glasses. In the USA and many other countries the Pfund Colour Grader is used to determine the grading.

The colour of honey is important in helping the large-scale producers to achieve a standard blend of each type of honey each year. Light coloured honeys are usually priced rather higher than the darker ones.

HISTORY OF HONEY

The evidence of man's efforts to acquire honey can be found in cave drawings such as one at Bicorpin in Eastern Spain, which dates back to 7,000 BC, showing a hunter about to take a comb from a bees' nest. Another, in Valencia, shows a hole in a cliff with bees flying round while two men climb ropes in an attempt to get the honey. A rock painting in India, dating back to 5,000 BC, shows honey being collected.

Honey was almost the only available sweetener and was eaten and appreciated by most of the old civilisations, among them the Ancient Egyptians who also used it for embalming the dead. Many primitive tribes used honey in their rain magic rites.

Honey production was an important rural industry of the Old Roman Empire. One of their sacrificial cakes, 'Libum', was made with honey.

The Arabians quoted honey in a proverb concerning their philosophy about life:

'Yuam asal, yuam basal . . . '
(Some days it's honey, Some days it's onions . . .)

Honey is mentioned in many of the old writings, in the Sanskrit, in the Koran and the Bible. In his poetic 'Song', King Solomon likened the lips of his beloved to the honeycomb and in Proverbs he advised his son to eat honey 'because it is good'.

There are many drinks to be made with honey which are both delicious and health-giving. The most well known, however, is a mixture of honey and water which was drunk in Ancient Rome, in Egypt and Ireland, India and Greece, where it was

said to be the liquor of the gods. (Even the angels were said to quench their thirst by sipping it.) A drink much praised by Roman gourmets was known as 'Muslem', made of honey, wine and water, well mixed and boiled. In ancient times, the Russians drank 'Lipez', made from the honey produced by the flowers of the linden tree. Ethiopians drank a honey brew called 'Tej' which was non-intoxicating and provided them with great energy.

The ancient Britons ate a great deal of honey, a fact which so impressed the Phoenecians when they arrived to trade in copper and tin that they called Britain 'The Isle of Honey'.

An old Scottish favourite to be taken 'a little and often', was 'Atholl Brose' made from equal parts of Ling honey, cream and mature whisky.

Mead was always regarded as a traditional drink of England, having been a great favourite of the Kings and their nobles, the Lords of the Manor, the peasants and serfs alike. Saxon Lords of the Manor accepted it as part payment of the rents due to them. There is a record that 10 dolias (large earthenware jars) was paid to King Ina of Sussex in AD 688. Honey was paid as rent and tribute in many other parts of the world, too. Honey remained an important food for a thousand years. Sugar, as a food or sweetener, was a luxury in Britain until the 17th century.

Bees were kept in monasteries everywhere, though not only for the honey. The beeswax for making candles was an important produce of the hive for the monks, and they were noted for their skill in producing mead—as some orders still are.

As time went on, swarms of bees were given as gifts and dowries; when his daughter was born, the Reverend Charles Butler, the grandfather of Gilbert White the naturalist of Selborne in Hampshire, gave her a swarm of bees.

When man first began to gather honey, he took it from wherever the bees had made their nests. Then, for easier access to the honey, he started to build hives for them composed of strips of bark bound to form cylinders. Sticks were wedged inside as foundations for the comb. When the honey was ready to be taken, the bees were smoked out, the bark pieces broken apart and the comb removed.

In South America, gourds were used, and coconut shells in Indonesia. Clay hives were made in Ancient Greece. Hives in Ethiopia were constructed of mud, straw and dung. Skeps composed of twisted straw were used not only in Britain but all over Europe. Bee-holes, which were special niches to protect the delicate straw creations, were constructed in walls and against the sides of houses. In some parts of Europe, holes were cut in the trunks of trees, a method still practised in the New Forest in Britain as late as the 1920s.

The breakthrough in bee-management came in 1852 when Lorenzo Lorraine Langstroth, a minister of Philadelphia in the USA, designed a new bee hive: a rectangular wooden box in which removable frames were fitted where the bees could build their wax combs. The Langstroth hive is still in use today and more widely favoured than any other type.

HONEY FOLKLORE

Folklore is filled with strange and wonderful beliefs about bees and the honey they make. The bee was regarded as sacred in many civilisations, so it is inevitable that their produce would be valued and believed to possess protective and miraculous powers.

Before it was realised that bees gathered nectar from flowers in order to make their honey, it was generally believed that they flew to Paradise and collected it from the Celestial Garden.

According to Mohammed, the bee was the only creature that was ever spoken to by God. The Greeks believed honey was the 'food of the gods'. They offered it to their deities and the baby Zeus was said to have lived on milk and honey while he lay hidden in a cave in Crete where his mother Rhea had taken him to save him from his murderous father, Kronos. Socrates' lips were touched with honey while he was an infant.

Honey was used in the rituals of birth, marriage and death, to provide food for the journeying soul and to preserve the body that it left behind.

In some civilisations, honey was regarded as a symbol of fertility and played an important part in weddings; drinks and cakes were made of it for the marriage feasts. In Greece, a girl was given a spoonful of honey by her new mother-in-law on her way home from her wedding so that only sweet words would pass her lips during her married life.

To ensure that everything would be sweet and harmonious, gipsies smeared the doorposts of their caravans with honey before a bridal couple entered. In India the breasts of a bride were touched with honey, while the Brahmins of Bengal annointed the girl's forehead, lips, eyelids and earlobes with honey to ward off evil spirits as well as to ensure that the marriage would be a happy one.

In certain African tribes, only honey and water was given to a mother after the birth of her child, and after the circumcision rites boys were given nothing but honey and water for a week. According to Hindu custom, as soon as a child was born, its tongue was smeared with honey. In many countries it was once the custom to give a new-born baby sips of honey and water as a protection against the devil.

Many of these customs contain far more common sense than superstition and they link naturally with the remedies that were used for specific health problems. (See pages 44 to 50.)

KEEPING AND STORING HONEY

The shelf-life of honey is said by the trade to be about $2\frac{1}{2}$ years, but in fact honey never goes bad, though as time passes the delicate flavour and aroma it had when first taken from the hive tends to disappear, and it may darken. A jar of honey found in one of the Egyptian tombs was quite black but it still retained its taste and scent after over 3,000 years.

Honey should be stored in a cool dry place in stone, glass, plastic or earthenware jars, never in metal containers as a chemical reaction is set up by the contact of the honey with the metal. The jars should be kept sealed to prevent fermentation of the honey. Strong-flavoured honeys tend to remain in prime condition the longest.

All honey will granulate after a time, though this varies from one honey to another and different types of honey will produce different granules, depending on the plant from which the nectar was gathered.

Honey kept in a cold place will granulate quickly because the least soluable sugars contained in it start to crystalise in a low temperature. So never freeze honey, for although it will not spoil either the flavour or the aroma it will hasten granulation.

Granulation can be prevented by pasteurising the honey but the heat needed to do so will destroy many of the valuable constituents. If for some reason you do need to heat it, the temperature should not exceed 40°F.

Coarse-grained honey can be 'seeded' by adding a small quantity of finely grained honey. When warmed, the granules in the mixture will become uniform.

The Owl and the Pussy-cat went to sea
In a beautiful pea-green boat.
They took some honey and plenty of money
Wrapped up in a five-pound note.

Edward Lear, *The Owl and the Pussy-cat*

HINTS ON USING HONEY

* Honey is much better for you than sugar but don't forget that it is sweeter. When substituting honey for sugar in a recipe, as a general rule, 1 tablespoonful of honey equals 3 of sugar. One cup of honey has the same volume as 1 cup of sugar but weighs $1\frac{1}{2}$ times as much, so reduce the liquid content in the recipe by one quarter: i.e. three-quarters of a cup instead of 1 cup.

* When buying honey make sure it is not liquid on top, with pale crystals on the bottom of the jar. This honey will have been spoiled by separation or fermentation because the water content is too high. Either return the jar to the shop or supplier, or use the honey for cooking.

* As a general guide, use light coloured honeys for cakes, biscuits and for sweetening fruit, cereals, puddings and tisanes. Darker honeys are best for gingerbread, fruit cakes and anything containing chocolate.

* Use honey to sweeten stewed fruit but never cook it with the fruit. Stir it in afterwards while the fruit is still warm. This will not destroy the value of the honey.

* Cakes made with honey instead of sugar will keep well. Honey helps baked food to stay soft and also improves both flavour and texture, but bake in a slower oven: decrease the temperature by 25°F.

* Add honey to the yeast instead of sugar when making bread: 2 teaspoons of honey to ¾oz yeast, for wholemeal bread. The loaves will keep better and remain moist.

* When adding honey to creamed butter, always drip it in very slowly, blending it in as you go.

* When measuring honey, first dip the spoon into hot water. The honey will then drip off easily.

* Honey can be made more liquid by warming it, and thicker by cooling. To liquidise honey which has granulated, stand the jar in a bowl of hot (never boiling) water. Once liquid, the honey is not likely to granulate again but if it does, the granules will be smaller.

* Honey mixes easily with liquids, warm and cold, and can be made to pour easily, perhaps as a sauce for fruit or cereal, by thinning it with a little water.

* Remember that honey will lower the freezing point of water in which it has been dissolved.

RECIPES WITH HONEY

There are many traditional cakes and confections made with honey, among them Halvah and Baklava of Greece and Turkey, Nougat and *Pain d'épice* of France and *Lebkuchen* of Germany. But honey can be used for other food beside sweet cakes. It is perfect for basting meat, for cooking with fish, and for giving vegetables a new and delicious flavour. It can be included in sauces, in salad dressings and used as a glaze.

HONEY WITH MEAT

HONEYED LAMB CUTLETS

Honey sauce goes perfectly with lamb and turns an ordinary dish into something very special.

4 lamb cutlets
a little cooking oil
1 level dessertspoon plain flour
juice of ½ lemon
1 dessertspoon honey
4 fl oz stock
small gherkins, to garnish

Brush the cutlets with the oil and place under a hot grill to brown on both sides. Reduce the heat and grill until the cutlets are cooked. Set aside and keep warm.

Using a dessertspoonful of the fat from the grill pan, stir in the flour, and cook over low heat until brown, then blend in the lemon juice, honey and stock. Cook over brisk heat for about 3 minutes, stirring all the time.

Pour the sauce over the cutlets, coating each carefully, and serve garnished with sliced gherkins.

For 2

GLAZE FOR HONEY ROAST HAM

For a really special Honey Roast Ham try this following glaze.

cloves
2 tablespoons honey
2 tablespoons fresh orange juice

Bake the ham in the usual way, remove the rind and score the meat with criss-cross lines to form squares. Stick a clove in the centre of each square and pour over the combined honey and orange juice. Return to the oven, 400°F (200°C) Gas 6, and bake for about 15 minutes, basting frequently, until the ham is nicely glazed.

HONEY GLAZE FOR ROAST LAMB

All plain cuts of meat can be glazed with honey while roasting. It also gives the meat an attractive appearance.

1 tablespoon honey
1 teaspoon orange juice
1 teaspoon lemon juice
chopped mint, to serve

Roast the lamb according to your taste, but 15 minutes before the end of cooking time drain off the fat from the baking dish and pour the combined honey, orange and lemon juice over the meat. Return the meat to the oven and baste frequently till the end of cooking time.

Add the chopped mint to the pan juices and serve separately as a sauce.

HONEY WITH FISH

TROUT AND ALMONDS
WITH HONEY SAUCE

An unusual and delicious sauce for trout.

3 medium-sized trout, cleaned
seasoned flour
3 oz butter
1½ oz almonds
juice of ½ lemon
1 tablespoon honey

Coat the trout with flour. Melt half the butter in a
pan and fry the fish for about 5 minutes each side, till
cooked. Place on a dish and keep hot.

Add the remaining butter to the pan and fry the
almonds until golden brown, then remove and keep
hot. Stir the lemon juice into the pan, add the honey
and let it bubble for minute, then pour over the trout
and spoon the almonds on top.

For 3

BLACK BUTTER AND HONEY SAUCE FOR MACKEREL

An excellent sauce to serve with hot or cold mackerel. Mackerel is a bland-tasting fish and really needs something to give it extra interest.

4 oz butter
sprig of parsley, chopped fine
2 tablespoons wine vinegar
1 tablespoon honey

Melt the butter in a small saucepan and allow it to brown, being careful not to burn it. Add the parsley and cook for a few seconds, then remove the pan from the heat. Add the wine vinegar and the honey and stir.

HONEY WITH VEGETABLES

Toss young peas or root vegetables in a little butter and a couple of spoonfuls of honey after cooking for a lovely flavour and finish.

GLAZED POTATOES OR ONIONS

The following recipe shows how it is done with root vegetables. Quite delicious.

2 oz butter
2 dessertspoons honey

Cook the potatoes or onions in boiling salted water till tender. Melt the butter in a pan and stir in the honey. Drain the potatoes or onions, place in a baking dish and pour the glaze over them. Bake in a moderate oven, 350°F (180°C) Gas 4, till browned and nicely glazed.

Carrots can be cooked in the same way, adding 1 teaspoon orange rind and 1 teaspoon lemon rind, very finely grated, to the glaze.

HONEYED CARROTS

4 large or 6 medium carrots
2 oz butter
1 dessertspoon dry mustard powder
2 tablespoons honey
1 tablespoon chopped almonds

Peel and slice the carrots and cook in fast boiling salted water till tender.

Meanwhile, combine the butter, mustard powder and honey in a small pan. Cook for about 3 minutes, stirring continually.

Drain the carrots, pour the sauce over them and sprinkle with the chopped almonds.

HONEY SWEETS AND PUDDINGS

HONEY PUDDING

Delicious served with custard or cream, marbled with honey.

1 oz semolina
¼ pint milk
6 oz fresh white breadcrumbs
4 oz honey
grated rind of 1 lemon
1 teaspoon ground ginger
1 oz butter, melted
2 eggs, separated

Cook the semolina in the milk for 10 minutes, then pour over the breadcrumbs. Add the honey, finely grated lemon rind, the ginger, the melted butter and the egg yolks and mix well.

Whisk the egg whites until stiff and fold into the mixture. Pour into a bowl and steam for about 2 hours.

For 4

BAKED PEARS WITH HONEY

Try adding chopped nuts to the filling for a special pudding. Honey is the ideal sweetener for pears.

4 pears
3 tablespoons honey
$\frac{1}{2}$ oz butter
small pinch ground cloves

Peel, halve and core the pears. Place inner sides up in a baking dish and fill the centres with $\frac{1}{2}$ tablespoon honey and a tiny knob of butter. Sprinkle sparingly with ground cloves.

Make a syrup by stirring 1 tablespoon honey into $\frac{1}{2}$ cup of hot water and pour into the dish around the pears. Bake in a moderate oven, 350°F (180°C) Gas 4, for 20–30 minutes, basting occasionally.

Serve hot with cream.

For 4

HONEY SOUFFLÉ

Simple and delicious.

4 eggs
¼ pint double cream
6 tablespoons honey

Separate the eggs and whip the whites until stiff. Beat the cream until it is thick.

Mix the egg yolks and the honey and place in the top of a double saucepan. Stir over boiling water until the mixture thickens. Do not let it boil.

Allow to cool, then fold in the egg whites and the cream. Serve very cold.

For 4

HONEY DELIGHT

This is a version of the famous Atholl Brose.

1 level tablespoon fine oatmeal
½ pint double cream
3 tablespoons clear honey
juice and grated rind of 1 lemon

Lightly toast the oatmeal in a small saucepan over a low flame. Beat the cream until smooth but not too thick. Without over-heating it, melt the honey and fold it into the cream, then stir in the lemon juice and the oatmeal.

Serve in tall glasses sprinkled with the finely grated lemon peel.

For 4

EASY CHEESECAKE WITH HONEY

A spectacular end to a special meal.

1½ cups digestive biscuit crumbs
½ cup chopped nuts
3 oz butter, melted
3 eggs
3 cups cottage cheese, sieved and creamed
¼ cup caster sugar
¼ cup pale honey
squeeze of lemon juice
whipped cream and soft fruit to decorate

Combine the biscuit crumbs, nuts and butter and press into an 8-inch greased sandwich tin, preferably with a removable base. Put into the fridge to chill.

Beat the eggs and add, a little at a time, to the cheese, then stir in the sugar, honey and lemon juice. Beat until smooth, then spread on to the crumb crust.

Bake in a hot oven, 400°F (200°C) Gas 6, for 20 minutes, then cool and remove from the tin.

Serve topped with whipped cream and decorated with soft fruit.

For 6–8

HONEY CAKES
AND BISCUITS

HONEY TARTLETS

6 oz plain flour
pinch of salt
4 oz butter
1 egg yolk, beaten
½ cup sour cream

For the filling:
honey
caster sugar
chopped walnuts

Sift together the flour and the salt and rub in the butter. Add the well-beaten egg yolk and the sour cream, and mix.

Leave the pastry in a cold place for about 1 hour. Roll out the pastry, cut into rings and line well-greased tart or patty tins with it. Fill each one with 1 teaspoon each of honey, caster sugar and chopped walnuts.

Bake in a hot oven, 400°F (200°C) Gas 6, for about 15 minutes, until the pastry edges are golden brown. Serve hot or cold, with cream.

ICED LEMON CAKE

4 oz butter
6 oz pale honey
2 eggs, beaten
8 oz self-raising flour
pinch of salt
½ teaspoon bicarbonate of soda
rind of 1 lemon, finely grated
a little milk
2 tablespoons lemon juice
glacé cherries to decorate

For the icing and filling:
3 oz icing sugar
2 oz butter
juice of ½ lemon

Cream the butter, dribble in the honey and add the well-beaten eggs. Sift the flour, salt and bicarbonate of soda together and mix in the lemon rind, then stir into the creamed mixture, a little at a time. Add enough milk to make a smooth firm consistency, then pour in 2 tablespoons of lemon juice and beat well.

Divide the mixture between two well-greased 8-inch sandwich tins and bake in a moderate oven, 350°F (180°C) Gas 4, for 25 minutes, until firm and golden. Turn on to a wire rack to cool.

Mix the icing ingredients, thinning with a little honey if liked, and spread on the cake. Decorate with glacé cherries.

HONEY BISCUITS

If liked, these biscuits can be sandwiched together with the cream filling used in the previous recipe.

4 oz butter
½ cup sugar
1 egg, well beaten
⅓ cup honey
2 cups plain flour
¼ teaspoon cinnamon
1 teaspoon baking powder
pinch of salt

Cream the butter and sugar and add the beaten egg and the honey. Sift the dry ingredients and fold into the creamed mixture. Roll into small balls, place on a well-greased baking tray and flatten with a fork. Bake at 350°F (180°C) Gas 4 for 10–15 minutes.

Makes 30 to 40

HONEY FINGERS

1 cup rolled oats, fine oatmeal or Rice Krispies
1 tablespoon each honey, cream, grated nuts
a few dates, chopped

Mix all the ingredients together and spread on greaseproof paper to form an oblong about ¼ inch thick. Chill well, then cut into finger-shaped lengths.
   Delicious served with stewed fruit or ice cream.

Makes about 24 fingers

SAUCES AND SALAD DRESSINGS WITH HONEY

HAZELNUT HONEY SAUCE

A lovely crunchy sauce to serve with ice cream.

2 oz hazelnuts
2 oz unsalted butter
3 level tablespoons honey
1 oz soft brown sugar
1 tablespoon lemon juice
1 tablespoon water

Gently heat the hazelnuts in a small pan, turn them into a clean teacloth and rub off the brown skins and grate coarsely.

Heat the butter gently, taking care not to let it brown. Add the nuts and fry till just beginning to change colour. Remove from heat and stir in all the other ingredients. When well mixed, return to the heat to amalgamate everything.

37

APPLE SAUCE WITH HONEY

Delicious hot or cold with pork or poultry.

6 green apples, peeled, cored and chopped
½ cup each honey and water
juice of ½ lemon
3 cloves

Place the honey, water, lemon juice and cloves in a pan and bring slowly to the boil. Add the apple pieces and cover the pan. Simmer very gently till the apples are soft, then remove the cloves.

SALAD DRESSING

As a variation try using 2 tablespoons cider vinegar instead of the lemon juice and adding some finely chopped fresh mint instead of the paprika and garlic.

½ cup good olive oil
½ cup lemon juice
½ cup clear, pale honey
pinch of paprika
½ teaspoon salt
1 clove garlic, crushed

Place all the ingredients in a jar, cover tightly and shake well before using.

This will keep for several days in a fridge, but do not freeze. Makes about 1½ cups of dressing.

PRESERVES

HONEY, MINT AND APPLE JELLY

Delicious with roast lamb or pork and all cold meat.

4 lb windfall apples
2 handfuls fresh mint
1½ lb honey
½ pint vinegar
green food colouring (optional)

Cut up the apples (there is no need to peel them) and place in a pan with the mint and ½ pint water. Cover the pan and cook till the apples are soft.

Mash the pulp through a sieve and add the honey and vinegar. Return to the pan, bring to the boil and boil fast for 5 minutes. The jelly can be coloured with a little green food colouring if preferred. Pour it into hot sterilised jars and cover.

Makes about 6 pounds of jelly

HONEY AND...

Honey is delicious eaten with:

* Muesli
* Rolled oats with chopped apricots and a little milk or cream
* On cereals instead of sugar—much better for you, too
* Hot oatcakes, scones, toasted tea-cakes or crumpets
* Poured over ice cream
* Puddings and pies
* Mixed with cream cheese as a spread
* And of course there's nothing quite like honey spread on bread and butter. As one poet wrote so enthusiastically:

'Of all the meals you can buy with money
Give me wholemeal bread and honey . . .'

DELICIOUS DRINKS
MADE WITH HONEY

MEAD

To make good mead is a long process and it needs knowledge and patience as there are many rules to be observed and the process cannot be hurried. However, there is a honey drink which can be made without any trouble. It does not need to be fermented, and there's no reason why you shouldn't call it mead if you wish to.

Dissolve 2 lbs of good honey in 4 pints of water. Boil the mixture over a gentle heat till the liquid is reduced to 3 pints. Pour into a bowl and cover. Leave for 2 or 3 days, then bottle.

There's also an old recipe from the County of Sussex which is known as mead: this one does need to be fermented. Bring 16 pints of water and 6 lbs honey slowly to the boil and add cinnamon, ginger, mace and cloves to taste.

Simmer gently till the liquor is reduced to 6 pints, and pour into an earthenware pot. When cool, add $\frac{1}{2}$ pint of yeast.

After fermentation subsides, pour into a wooden cask and close the bung. Keep for at least 12 months before using. It is mildly alcoholic.

SPICED MILK-SHAKE WITH HONEY

2 cups milk
2 tablespoons honey
pinch of cinnamon
scant pinch of ground ginger

Combine all ingredients in a blender and blend till frothing.

Makes one generous milk-shake

ICED COFFEE WITH HONEY

half a cinnamon stick
2 cups strong black coffee, very hot
2 tablespoons honey
crushed ice
whipped cream

Place the cinnamon stick in a jug and pour on the hot coffee. Leave to get cold.

Remove the cinnamon stick and stir in the honey.

Crush some ice and half fill two glasses. Pour in the coffee and top with whipped cream.

For 2

ORANGE AND HONEY DRINK

½ cup fresh orange juice
1 egg
1 tablespoon honey

Put all the ingredients in a blender and whizz for a minute.
This quantity is enough for one.

HONEY-MINT SUMMER DRINK

1 pint boiling water
6 tablespoons fresh mint, finely chopped
3 dessertspoons honey
½ cup lemon juice

Pour the boiling water over the mint, and leave to infuse until cold. Strain and add the honey and lemon juice and dilute to taste with ice-cold water.

HONEY TEA

But the most cooling drink in the whole world, according to the chef of a well-known London hotel, writing to a national newspaper during the 1920s, could be made as follows: 'Take a tumbler and put in 3 or 4 lumps of ice. Pour on hot tea. Leave to get cold. Add honey to taste and 2 slices of lemon.'

HONEY REMEDIES

The curative power of honey has been known for thousands of years and many of the old remedies are still very effective.

Hippocrates advised eating honey if you wished to live a long life and Democritus is said to have lived to the age of 109 with the aid of honey. According to Plutarch, the longevity of the Ancient Britons was entirely due to the amount of honey they consumed. He wrote: 'These Britons only begin to grow old at one hundred and twenty years of age ...' And it is no myth that the bee-keepers of Azerbaijan in the Caucasus live to a 100 and even 150 years.

During the Middle Ages, honey was used to treat boils, wounds, ulcers and burns. Sword cuts were dressed with honey and cobwebs. Honey was used throughout history, not only for its curative but also for its restorative power. RAF pilots were given

honey during the Battle of Britain to help them bear the strain of frequent flying.

Honey was given to Greek athletes of the past, and is still given to the athletes of today. Because the glucose it contains does not need to be digested but passes directly into the bloodstream, it is the ideal pick-me-up to take *during* strenuous exercise.

Honey is pure, soothing, non-irritant, safe, comparatively cheap, and antiseptic; no bacteria can survive in it. It is a gentle laxative; is effective for dressing burns and abrasions; for treating cuts and bruises; for respiratory problems and diseases of the lungs. It soothes a cough and eases a sore throat. It helps to keep the heart healthy.

Many of the following remedies are easy to make, pleasant to use and cost very little. They can be kept for a limited time in a cool place such as a shelf in the fridge. Some will keep well on the kitchen shelf or in the bathroom. The honey content in them prevents them going bad.

* If a jar of honey is held under the nose of someone suffering from an asthma attack, his breathing will grow easier.

* As a quick remedy for a painful steam burn, apply a little pure honey on a light dressing and lie it on the burn. Bandage lightly.

A REMEDY FOR SUNBURN

Mix: 2 tablespoons liquid honey
         2 tablespoons glycerine
         2 tablespoons lemon juice
         1 tablespoon toilet water

Use: Put all the ingredients into a glass jar, screw on the lid and shake. Apply as needed.

TO EASE A SORE THROAT OR A TROUBLESOME COUGH

Mix: 2 tablespoons honey
        2 tablespoons glycerine
        2 tablespoons lemon juice

Use: Warm the mixture and take a teaspoon as needed.

REMEDY FOR A COUGH

Mix: 1 teaspoon honey
        pinch nutmeg

Use: Take as required.

ANTISEPTIC HONEY GARGLE

*1 pint water
a good handful of chopped sage leaves, freshly gathered
if possible
1 tablespoon honey
scant pinch of cayenne pepper*

Pour boiling water over the sage and leave to stand for 10–15 minutes.

Strain and stir in the honey and cayenne pepper. Use warm, as required. It is a very soothing gargle.

HONEY FOR COLDS

Place a whole lemon in the oven and roast it till the peel starts to crack. Squeeze out 1 teaspoonful of the juice and mix with 1 teaspoonful of honey dissolved in a little warm water.

Repeat every half an hour.

A once-popular remedy for chills and colds was a drink known as 'hum', which was made from the washings of the combs after the honey had been extracted. It was seasoned with pepper. Fletcher, a man who once lived in Sussex, wrote:

> 'What a cold I have over my stomach
> Would that I had some hum!'

HONEY FOR HEALTHY ARTERIES AND CIRCULATION

As a general remedy, add lemon peel and pure honey to warm water and leave to soak for 3–4 hours then strain and bottle. Take 2 teaspoonfuls of the liquid every day for 3 months. Then discontinue for 2 months and repeat.

Used regularly, honey helps to maintain the correct balance of red corpuscles.

HONEY REMEDIES FOR SLEEPLESSNESS

* Stir 1 or 2 teaspoonfuls of pure honey into a glass of milk, just warmed, (not hot or boiling) and drink just before going to bed. The milk can be cold during the summer if preferred.
* Whisky, water and honey is also an effective soporific.
* A tisane of rosemary sweetened with a teaspoonful of honey is also helpful.
* If you wake in the night, take a teaspoonful of honey, or drink water sweetened with honey.

HONEY FOR INSTANT ENERGY

Not only did the athletes of Ancient Greece take honey to give them energy, but the Sherpa porters of the Himalayas eat honey to provide them with the staying power they need.

For a quick pick-me-up, either take a teaspoon of pure honey, or drink a glass of milk or water in which honey has been stirred.

HONEY TO BUILD RESISTANCE

Honey helps you to resist coughs and colds and flu. Eat oatmeal and honey mixed with a little milk as a daily health food to help you resist infection.

A REMEDY FOR HANGOVERS

Mix: 1 dessertspoon of honey
       juice of 1 lemon
       a little water

Use: Take as necessary.

A HEALTH DRINK

Mix: ½ cup milk
       ½ cup plain yoghurt
       1 dessertspoon of clear honey

Use: Drink every day—it is delicious and full of goodness.

HONEY TO RELIEVE HAYFEVER

Chew honeycomb five times a day for two days, then three times a day for as long as you need it. If possible, start the treatment 3 or 4 months before the attacks are likely to begin, thus preventing them.

Alternatively, chew honeycomb once a day and take 2 teaspoonfuls of honey at each meal.

The greatest benefit will be derived with honey and wax cappings, in combination.

HONEY FOR WEIGHTWATCHERS

Overweight people need not avoid eating honey.
Both fats and sugars contain energy-producing foods
which are burned up by contact with oxygen to
create energy. Sugars burn more rapidly than fats
and also produce energy far more quickly. Thus,
when honey containing its valuable sugars is
absorbed into the bloodstream, it will cause a rapid
burning up of fat, creating the energy needed to
continue the good work.

HONEY FOR BEAUTY

As a beautifier, honey is unique. It was used by
such famous beauties as Cleopatra and the
Queen of Sheba. Beauty-specialist, Barbara
Cartland, strongly recommends it.

Lotions and creams made with honey not only
pamper and improve the appearance of the skin, but
nourish and preserve it, too. Honey attracts and
holds moisture and is particularly good for people
with dry skin. It is also invaluable for people who
need to wear a lot of make-up.

A QUICK FACE MASK

For a quick and marvellously effective face mask dip your fingers in warm water, then into pure honey and gently massage into the face and neck. If you have a greasy skin, add a few drops of lemon juice to the honey. Leave for 20 minutes, then wash off with warm water.

A GOOD NOURISHING LOTION

Mix: 1 egg yolk
         1 teaspoon honey
         1 teaspoon glycerine

Use: Smear over the face and the neck and leave for 2 hours. Remove with warm water. Repeat the treatment twice a week.

This lotion will keep for 2 or 3 days in a cool place.

A CLEANSING AND NOURISHING FACE MASK

Mix: equal parts of honey, egg yolk, sour cream or fine oatmeal

Use: Apply liberally and leave on for 20 minutes, before washing off with warm water.

This treatment will soften and feed the skin, and will absorb any impurities to cleanse it thoroughly.

To Firm The Skin
Round The Eyes

Mix: 1 teaspoon honey
        1 egg white, well beaten

Use: Smooth it on gently and leave for 30 minutes.
        Rinse off with warm water.

To gain the full benefit, this treatment should be
done regularly.

A Quick Cleanser

Mix: 1 tablespoon clear honey with 1 pint water

Use: Dip a ball of cotton wool into the cleanser and
        smooth it over the face and neck. Leave it on
        for 10 minutes if you have time, then rinse
        with warm water.

This mixture can also be used as a conditioner for the
hair. Use before the final rinse.

In his *Primitive Physic, or an Easy and Natural
Method of Curing Most Diseases,* which was
published in 1830, John Wesley advised honey for
curing baldness and making hair grow. 'Rub the part
morning and evening with onions till red and rub it
afterwards with honey . . .'

A Lotion To Keep Hair Healthy

Mix: 4 oz honey
2 oz olive oil

Use: Place ingredients into a bottle and shake well.
Dip the tips of the fingers into the mixture
and massage the scalp for several minutes.
Wrap the head in a warm towel and leave on
for 20 minutes, then wash the hair as usual.

The lotion will keep well if stored in a cool dark
place. The treatment should be repeated every 3
months or every 6 weeks for dry lifeless hair. Queen
Anne is said to have found this lotion extremely
good.

Nourishing Hand Lotion

4 oz pure honey
4 oz cucumber juice
½ cup vodka

Pour the cucumber juice and vodka into a bottle, seal
and store in a dark place for just over 1 week. Then
filter the liquor through fine muslin and stir in the
honey. Apply once a day.

This can also be used for the face and neck and
should be left on for several hours for maximum
benefit.

FOR CHAPPED HANDS

Mix: *1 egg white*
       1 teaspoon glycerine
       1 dessertspoon honey
       a little cornflour to thicken

Use: Massage gently into the hands until completely absorbed.

FOR ROUGH, HARD SKIN

Mix: *½ teaspoon honey*
       1 tablespoon lemon juice

Use: Massage feet, knees and elbows with this lotion, then rinse off with warm water.

HONEY CREAM

Mix: *4 oz pure lard*
       2 egg yolks
       1 tablespoon honey
       1 tablespoon ground almonds
       a few drops almond essence

Use: Soften the lard and add the egg yolks. Beat in the rest of the ingredients and put into a screw-topped jar. Keep in a cool dark place. This cream is especially good massaged into work-worn hands, and for healing cracks and split cuticles.

AN ALL-PURPOSE LOTION

Mix: 1 dessertspoon clear honey
1 dessertspoon glycerine
1 dessertspoon lemon juice
1 dessertspoon elderflower water
1 small egg, well beaten

Use: Put everything into a jar and shake well to mix thoroughly. Leave on for 20 minutes and rinse off with warm or cold water. Apply regularly.

This is a lotion I've created for myself and which I find extremely good.

Elderflower water is specially beneficial for the complexion and can be made by pouring boiling water on to elderflowers. Leave for a few hours to steep, then strain. This water will keep quite well if a little Cologne is added to it. Elderflowers can be dried to ensure a regular supply. If you have no elderflowers, use rosewater instead.

A BEAUTY DRINK

As everyone knows, you must feel good inwardly if you want to look good outwardly.

Mix: 1 teaspoon honey
1 teaspoon lemon juice
1 teaspoon olive oil

Use: Take regularly before breakfast, if possible, to achieve a glowing vitality all day.

WORLD PRODUCTION OF HONEY

Honey is produced in almost every country in the world. Honey consumption is highest in Europe and in countries where Europeans have settled, such as Canada, the USA, Australia and New Zealand.

In 1983, world production was estimated at 897,000 tonnes. According to figures supplied by the countries of origin in spring 1983, the leading producers are:

USSR: 180,000 tonnes
China: 120,000 tonnes (1981)
USA: 100,300 tonnes
Mexico: 45,000 tonnes
Argentina: 33,000 tonnes

The three largest importing countries in the world are West Germany, Japan, and the UK. As the leading importer, West Germany obtains honey from Mexico, China, the Argentine and the Soviet Union. Much of this honey is also re-exported. In 1981, 12,986 tonnes were marketed.

Australia has now become one of the leading honey exporting countries in the world, the exports ranging from 5,000 to 11,000 tonnes (or 35,000,000–50,000,000 lbs) a year, depending on the weather conditions during the productive season. About 80% of this goes to the UK, the rest to over 30 countries including Japan.

Australia and Canada are in the lead in production of yield per hive, with Argentina and Mexico following, and although China is one of the highest producers in the world, the output per colony is less than half that of Canada's produce per hive.

The average annual honey crop in New Zealand is 6,000 tonnes. The New Zealanders are the greatest honey eaters in the world. New Zealand also exports her honey. In a seven-year average, 1973–1979 for example, 45% of the honey went to Japan, 21% to the UK, 19% to the EEC, 7% to the Middle East and 8% to other countries.

In Britain, honey is very much a cottage industry and bee-keeping is not confined only to the rural areas. It has been estimated that the honey yield in towns, and in London in particular, actually exceeds that of the country areas. This is partly due to the fact that there are fewer poisonous sprays and insecticides to kill both the bees and the nectar-producing plants from which the honey is made. In 1976, a bee-keeper in Holland Park collected 800 lbs of honey from his four hives.

Honey is a world commodity and subject to control. Commercial bee-keepers and apiarists are registered. Honey exporters operate under licence and are reviewed regularly in many countries.

Packaging is carefully supervised. There are strict regulations regarding hygiene. Official requirements ensure that honey is in perfect condition at the port of discharge.

Research in the management of bees and the production of honey goes on all over the world. At Azerbaijan in the Caucasus where bee-keepers are known to have lived for as long as 150 years, some of the world's finest honey is now being produced in state bee farms where no chemical sprays are used. Funds are allocated by governments for research projects, and bee-keepers, both professional and amateur, are kept up to date with photographic libraries, books, films, video-cassettes, lectures and meetings.

Bee-keepers care about their bees not simply because honey is profitable, but also because the bee is a beautiful, mysterious, industrious little creature which has always fascinated mankind.

KEEPING BEES FOR HONEY

If you are not a bee-keeper you may want to become one, especially if you live in the country, but even if you live in the middle of a town a hive can be kept on an allotment or back garden, or even on a balcony. Before launching into the new project, do check that neither you nor anyone immediately around you is allergic to bee stings.

The best time to start bee-keeping, if you live in Britain, is during the spring when the growing season lies ahead, but don't be too ambitious. Start with a small colony which is known as a 'nucleus', and has a young fertile queen bee. Though there will not be much surplus honey in the first year, there will be ample opportunity to study the bees as the season goes on.

There are many laws concerning bee-keeping, so check with the local Department of Agriculture. Get the names and addresses of local Bee-Keeping Officers and join your nearest Bee-Keeping Association, which will give you advice about the hive and other basic equipment you will need, where to get it, and help you with any problems that may arise. They may also be able to advise you as where to get your 'nucleus', so that the source and characteristics of your bees will be known. And of course, you should get to know local bee-keepers, who will be only too willing to give you a helping hand if you need one. Bee people are always helpful about bees.

God made man
Man made money
God made bees
Bees make honey . . .

ACKNOWLEDGEMENTS

The Ministry of Agriculture and Fisheries

The Australian Honey Board

The Ministry of Agriculture and Fisheries, New Zealand

Instuto Mexicano de Comercio Exterior

Miss Margaret Ison, Bee-keeper, Treasurer of the West Sussex Bee-Keepers' Association and late Head of Science of Claremont School, who has given me a great deal of valuable information about both bees and honey

My sister Jone Budd, for all her help with research and testing recipes